DOMINICAN REPUBLIC 2016 HUMAN RIGHTS REPORT

EXECUTIVE SUMMARY

The Dominican Republic is a representative constitutional democracy. In May voters elected Danilo Medina of the Dominican Liberation Party (PLD) as president for a second four-year term. Impartial outside observers assessed the elections as generally free and orderly despite failures in the rollout of a new electronic voting system.

Civilian authorities at times did not maintain effective control over the security forces.

The most serious human rights problem was widespread discrimination against Haitian migrants and their descendants. In 2013 the Constitutional Tribunal ruled that Dominican-born descendants of individuals residing in the country without legal status, most of whom were of Haitian descent, were not entitled to Dominican citizenship and retroactively revoked their citizenship. The naturalization law, promulgated in 2014, helped restore citizenship rights to many of those affected, although the majority remained without nationality documents at year's end.

Other human rights problems included extrajudicial killings by security forces, overcrowded and dangerously substandard prison conditions, arbitrary arrest and detention, lengthy pretrial detention, weak rule of law, and impunity for corruption. There were also reports of chronic violence against women, including domestic violence, rape, and femicide; trafficking in persons; discrimination against persons based on sexual orientation or gender identity; and inadequate enforcement of labor laws.

The government took some steps to punish officials who committed human rights abuses, but there were widespread reports of official impunity and corruption, especially concerning officials of senior rank.

Section 1. Respect for the Integrity of the Person, Including Freedom from:

a. Arbitrary Deprivation of Life and other Unlawful or Politically Motivated Killings

There were numerous reports that the government or its agents committed arbitrary or unlawful killings. The National Human Rights Commission (NHRC) reported

more than 180 extrajudicial killings by police forces through September. The Attorney General's Office reported 74 extrajudicial killings through June.

Violence connected to the 2016 national elections resulted in six deaths, but there were no reports that government agents or security forces were involved in the violence. Prior to the elections, on March 11, an intrapolitical party conflict resulted in the killing of one man. Authorities arrested the alleged perpetrator who, as of November, was incarcerated pending trial. The attorney general alleged the incident arose from a dispute over the party's congressional candidate selection.

b. Disappearance

There were no reports of politically motivated disappearances during the year. The NHRC reported it was investigating six unresolved disappearance cases of human rights activists that occurred between 2009 and 2014, which they believed were politically motivated.

c. Torture and Other Cruel, Inhuman, or Degrading Treatment or Punishment

Although the law prohibits torture, beating, and physical abuse of detainees and prisoners, there were reports that security force members, primarily police, carried out such practices. The law provides penalties of 10 to 20 years' imprisonment for torture and physical abuse and sentences of up to 30 years for aggravated cases.

The NHRC reported that police used various forms of physical and mental abuse to obtain confessions from detained suspects. According to the NHRC, abusive methods used to extract confessions included suffocation by covering detainees' heads with plastic bags, hitting them with broom handles, forcing them to remain standing overnight, and hitting them in the ears with gloved fists or hard furniture foam so as not to leave marks. The Attorney General's Office stated it did not receive any formal complaints of torture during the year. In August the Attorney General's Office officially instructed local prosecutors to monitor prisoner treatment and allegations of torture.

Prison and Detention Center Conditions

Prison conditions ranged from compliance with international standards in "model" prisons or correctional rehabilitation centers (CRCs) to harsh and lacking adequate space and medical care in "traditional" prisons. Threats to life and health included communicable diseases, poor sanitation, poor access to health-care services, a lack of well-trained prison guards, and prisoners attacking other inmates. These problems were exacerbated in traditional prisons, which were severely overcrowded.

<u>Physical Conditions</u>: Gross overcrowding was a problem in traditional prisons. The NHRC reported that on average there were approximately 15,000 prisoners in traditional prisons and 10,000 in CRCs, a ratio constant over the past several years, as traditional prisons had not been phased out. La Victoria, the oldest traditional prison, held more than 8,000 inmates, although it was designed for a maximum capacity of 2,500. La Romana Prison was the only prison where facilities for male and female inmates were separated, but collocated.

Police and military inmates received preferential treatment, as did those with the financial means to rent preferential bed space and purchase other necessities.

According to the Directorate of Prisons, military and police personnel guarded traditional prisons, while a trained civilian guard corps provided security at CRCs. Reports of mistreatment and violence in prisons were common, as were reports of harassment, extortion, and inappropriate searches of prison visitors. Some prisons remained effectively outside the control of authorities, and there were allegations of drug and arms trafficking, prostitution, and sexual abuse within prisons. Wardens at traditional prisons often controlled only the perimeter, while inmates ruled the inside with their own rules and system of justice. The Attorney General's Office reported it received 15 complaints of prison abuse, determined four had merit, and prosecuted them.

Although the law mandates separation of prisoners according to severity of offense, authorities did not have the capability to do so. According to a 2014 estimate from the Directorate of Prisons, 62 percent of inmates in La Victoria, the largest traditional prison, were in preventive custody awaiting trial. The NHRC reported that some inmates remained in pretrial detention for up to three years. The National Office of Public Defense (NOPD) reported filing 788 motions through October to cease preventive custody.

Health and sanitary conditions were generally poor. Prisoners commonly slept on the floor because there were no beds available. Prison officials did not separate sick inmates. All prisons had infirmaries, but most infirmaries did not meet the needs of the prison population. In traditional prisons inmates had to purchase their own medications or rely on family members or other outside associates to deliver their medications. Most reported deaths were due to illnesses. From late February to March, a cholera outbreak in La Victoria resulted in 75 positive cases and four deaths. The National Tuberculosis Control Program reported that the Ministry of Health, in conjunction with the Attorney General's Office and the Directorate of Prisons, instituted a program to control the spread of tuberculosis in 32 prisons.

According to the Directorate for the Control of Sexually Transmitted Diseases and HIV/AIDS, 2 percent of the prison population was HIV-positive. The directorate reported that all prisons in the system provided on-site HIV/AIDS testing, treatment, and counseling services. According to the Directorate of Prisons, all prisons provided HIV/AIDS treatment, but the NHRC stated that, while CRCs were able to provide HIV/AIDS treatment, none of the traditional prisons was properly equipped to provide such treatment. In the case of the CRCs, some prisoners with mental disabilities received treatment, including therapy, for their conditions. The government did not provide services to prisoners with mental disabilities in traditional prisons. Neither CRCs nor traditional prisons provided access for persons with disabilities.

Administration: Recordkeeping in prisons was inadequate. Public defenders provided legal services to prisoners and in some cases assisted with certain complaints.

Independent Monitoring: The government permitted visits and monitoring by independently funded and operated nongovernmental organization (NGO) observers and media. The director of the NHRC served as a prisoner advocate. The NHRC, National Office of Public Defense, Attorney General's Office, and CRC prison administration together created human rights committees in each CRC with guaranteed surprise visit access for the committees. The committees exercised this right, including a June visit to La Victoria. Prisoners could submit complaints regarding their treatment verbally or in writing to the human rights committees and most often did so through family members, lawyers, or human rights defenders.

d. Arbitrary Arrest or Detention

The constitution prohibits detention without a warrant unless authorities apprehend a suspect during the commission of a criminal act or in other special circumstances but permits detention without charge for up to 48 hours. Arbitrary arrest and detention continued to be problems, and there were numerous reports of individuals held and later released with little or no explanation for the detention.

NGOs reported that many of the detainees were taken into custody at the scene of a crime or during drug raids. In many instances authorities fingerprinted, questioned, and then released those detainees.

Role of the Police and Security Apparatus

The Ministry of Interior and Police oversees the National Police, Tourist Police, and Metro Police. The Minister of Armed Forces directs the military, Airport Security Authority and Civil Aviation, Port Security Authority, and Border Security Corps. The National Department of Intelligence and the National Drug Control Directorate, which have personnel from both police and armed forces, report directly to the president.

Police operated in a dangerous environment. Gun ownership was widespread, and crime and homicides were common, especially in urban areas. The Attorney General's Office reported 74 extrajudicial killings through June, of which it prosecuted 18 cases. Authorities fired or prosecuted police officers found to have acted outside of established police procedures. The Internal Affairs Unit investigated charges of gross misconduct by members of the National Police. These cases involved physical or verbal aggression, threats, improper use of a firearm, muggings, and theft.

Training for military and the National Drug Control Directorate enlisted personnel and officers and the National Police included instruction on human rights. The Ministry of the Armed Forces provided human rights training or orientation to officers of various ranks as well as to civilians during the year. The Border Security Corps conducted mandatory human rights training at its training facilities for border officers. The Graduate School of Human Rights and International Humanitarian Rights trained civilians and armed forces personnel. The school also had programs in which members of the armed forces and civilians from Congress, district attorney offices, the Supreme Court, government ministries, the National Police, and the Central Electoral Board participated.

In July the government approved a police reform law to curb corruption, improve training, and increase transparency.

Arrest Procedures and Treatment of Detainees

The constitution provides that an accused person may be detained for up to 48 hours without a warrant before being presented to judicial authorities. The law also permits police to apprehend without an arrest warrant any person caught in the act of committing a crime or reasonably linked to a crime, such as in cases involving hot pursuit or escaped prisoners. Police sometimes detained suspects for investigation or interrogation longer than 48 hours. Police often detained all suspects and witnesses to a crime. Successful habeas corpus hearings reduced abuses of the law significantly. There was a functioning bail system. There was also a functioning system of house arrest.

The law requires provision of counsel to indigent defendants, although staffing levels were inadequate to meet demand. The NOPD represented defendants in approximately 80 percent of all criminal cases brought before the courts, although geographically they covered only 13 of 34 judicial districts. Many detainees and prisoners who could not afford private counsel did not have prompt access to a lawyer. Prosecutors and judges handled interrogations of juveniles, which the law prohibits by or in the presence of police.

Arbitrary Arrest: Police made sporadic sweeps or roundups in low-income, high-crime communities during which they arrested and detained individuals without warrants. During these sweeps police arrested large numbers of residents and seized personal property allegedly used in criminal activity. Through July the NOPD reported 525 cases of arbitrary arrest, based on their statistics of cases where authorities subsequently released defendants because of a lack of judicial authorization. The Attorney General's Office reported a decrease in arbitrary arrests connected to mass arrests at the scene of a crime due to training conducted in concert with human rights NGOs.

Pretrial Detention: Many suspects endured long pretrial detention. Under the criminal procedures code, a judge may order a detainee to remain in police custody between three and 18 months. According to the Directorate of Prisons, 62 percent of inmates were in pretrial custody. The average pretrial detention time was typically three months, but there were reports of cases of pretrial detention lasting up to three years. Time served in pretrial detention counted toward completing a sentence.

The failure of prison authorities to produce detainees for court hearings caused some trial postponements. Many inmates had their court dates postponed because they lacked transportation from prison to court or because their lawyer, codefendants, or witnesses did not appear. Despite additional protections for defendants in the criminal procedures code, in some cases authorities held inmates beyond the legally mandated deadlines although there were no formal charges against them.

<u>Detainee's Ability to Challenge Lawfulness of Detention before a Court</u>: Any prisoner detained for more than 48 hours without formal charges is entitled to file a motion of habeas corpus. The presiding judge at such a hearing is empowered to order the prisoner's release. The judge's decision to release a prisoner is subject to appeal by the district attorney.

<u>Protracted Detention of Rejected Asylum Seekers or Stateless Persons</u>: There were isolated cases of asylum seekers detained due to a lack of documentation (see sections 2.d. and 6).

e. Denial of Fair Public Trial

The law provides for an independent judiciary. Improper influence on judicial decisions, however, was widespread. Interference ranged from selective prosecution to dismissal of cases amid allegations of bribery or undue political pressure. The judiciary routinely dismissed high-level corruption cases during President Medina's five years in office. Corruption of the judiciary was also a serious problem (see section 4). The NOPD reported that the most frequent form of interference with judicial orders occurred when authorities refused to abide by writs of habeas corpus to free detainees.

Trial Procedures

The law provides for a presumption of innocence, the right to a defense in a fair and public trial, the right to confront or question witnesses, and the right against self-incrimination. Defendants have the right to be present and consult with an attorney in a timely manner, and the indigent have a right to a public defender. The law provides for free interpretation as necessary. The constitution also provides for the right to appeal and prohibits higher courts from increasing the sentences of lower courts.

The District Attorney's Office is required to notify the defendant and attorney of criminal charges as well as of evidence the office will present in court. Defendants and attorneys have access to government-held evidence and may confront adverse witnesses, but only after the preliminary hearing, when the judge has approved the indictment. Defendants have the right to present their own witnesses and evidence.

Military and police tribunals share jurisdiction over cases involving members of the security forces. While the tribunals have jurisdiction over cases involving violations of internal rules and regulations, civilian criminal courts handled cases of killings and other serious crimes allegedly committed by members of the security forces.

Political Prisoners and Detainees

There were no reports of political prisoners or detainees.

Civil Judicial Procedures and Remedies

There are separate court systems for claims under criminal law, commercial and civil law, and labor law. Commercial and civil courts reportedly suffered lengthy delays in adjudicating cases, although their decisions were generally enforced. As in criminal courts, undue political or economic influence in civil court decisions remained a problem.

Citizens had recourse to file an "amparo," an action to seek redress of any violation of a constitutional right, including violations of human rights protected by the constitution. This remedy was used infrequently and only by those with sophisticated legal counsel.

f. Arbitrary or Unlawful Interference with Privacy, Family, Home, or Correspondence

The law prohibits arbitrary entry into a private residence, except when police are in hot pursuit of a suspect, when a suspect is caught in the act of committing a crime, or if police suspect a life is in danger. The law provides that all other entries into a private residence require an arrest or search warrant issued by a judge. Police conducted illegal searches and seizures, however, including raids without warrants on private residences in many poor neighborhoods.

Although the government denied using unauthorized wiretaps, monitoring of private e-mail, or other surreptitious methods to interfere with the private lives of individuals and families, human rights groups and opposition politicians alleged that such interference continued. Opposition political parties alleged that government officials at times threatened subordinates with loss of employment and other benefits in order to compel them to support the incumbent PLD party and attend PLD campaign events. The NOPD reported incidents where police imprisoned family members of a suspect in order to compel the suspect to surrender. Individuals without access to citizenship documents were not able to vote, marry, or access education or other basic services.

Section 2. Respect for Civil Liberties, Including:

a. Freedom of Speech and Press

The constitution provides for freedom of speech and press, and the government generally respected these rights. The independent media were active and expressed a wide variety of views with some restriction.

Press and Media Freedoms: Individuals and groups were generally able to criticize the government publicly and privately without reprisal, although there were several incidents in which authorities intimidated journalists or other news professionals.

Violence and Harassment: Journalists and other persons who worked in media were occasionally harassed or physically attacked. The newspaper *El Dia* reported that journalists, specifically in rural areas, received threats for investigating or denouncing criminal groups or official corruption. The Inter American Press Association reported that journalists suffered violent attacks from military and police security details of government officials, particularly during public protests and riots.

Censorship or Content Restrictions: The constitution provides for protection of the confidentiality of journalists' sources and includes a "conscience clause" allowing journalists to refuse reporting assignments. Nonetheless, journalists practiced self-censorship, particularly when coverage could adversely affect the economic or political interests of media owners. Media outlets restricted the release of names of journalists covering stories connected to drug trafficking and other security matters in the interest of protecting them.

Libel/Slander Laws: The law criminalizes defamation and insult with harsher punishment for offenses committed against public or state figures than for offenses against private individuals. The Dominican College of Journalists reported that journalists were sued by politicians, private-sector and government officials, and criminal groups to pressure them to stop reporting. In February the Constitutional Tribunal annulled several articles from the Law on Freedom of Expression that had criminalized statements denouncing events that were of public interest and that authorities considered damaging. The court also ruled that media outlets, executive staff, and publishers are not liable for libel suits against individual journalists, thus easing some past pressure that business interests, which controlled much of the mainstream media, put on journalists. The law still penalizes libel for statements concerning the private lives of certain public figures, including government officials and foreign heads of state.

Internet Freedom

There were no government restrictions on access to the internet. According to the International Telecommunication Union, 52 percent of citizens used the internet in 2015.

Academic Freedom and Cultural Events

There were no government restrictions on academic freedom or cultural events.

b. Freedom of Peaceful Assembly and Association

Freedom of Assembly

The law provides for freedom of assembly. Outdoor public marches and meetings require permits, which the government usually granted. On several occasions police used force to disperse demonstrations and injured demonstrators and bystanders.

Freedom of Association

The law provides for freedom of association, and the government generally respected this right (see section 7.a.).

c. Freedom of Religion

See the Department of State's *International Religious Freedom Report* at www.state.gov/religiousfreedomreport/.

d. Freedom of Movement, Internally Displaced Persons, Protection of Refugees, and Stateless Persons

The law provides for freedom of internal movement, foreign travel, emigration, and repatriation, and the government generally respected these rights, with some exceptions. The government cooperated in a limited manner with the Office of the UN High Commissioner for Refugees (UNHCR) and other humanitarian organizations in providing protection and assistance to internally displaced persons, refugees, returning refugees, asylum seekers, stateless persons, or other noted persons of concern.

In 2014 the government promulgated a National Regularization Plan that enabled undocumented migrants in the country to apply for temporary legal residency. In January 2014 the government discontinued all deportations to give irregular migrants a chance to participate in this plan. The plan's application period closed in June 2015, and in August 2015 the government resumed deportations. In July the government extended the expiration date of the temporary resident cards issued under the plan.

The National Regularization Plan granted temporary residency status to approximately 250,000 irregular migrants (98 percent Haitian). According to census data, up to 280,000 Haitian migrants may not have applied or qualified for regularization and were subject to deportation. UN officials accompanied immigration authorities during interception procedures conducted in different provinces. According to the United Nations, the deportation procedures it observed were orderly, legal, and individualized, in compliance with applicable international human rights standards. The government invited the international community to observe and comment on deportations. The International Organization for Migration (IOM) reported that, as of September, the military patrolled the border and removed interdicted persons without individualized screening procedures, thus putting at risk other protected undocumented populations, including regularization plan beneficiaries, and undocumented Dominicans. In August the IOM counted 13 individuals with legal residency status who were detained pending removal and should have been protected from deportation. The IOM assisted these individuals to avoid deportation. The IOM also reported cases of individuals deported because authorities did not permit them to retrieve immigration or citizenship documents from their residences as well as deportations of women who left children behind in their residences.

Protection of Refugees

<u>Access to Asylum</u>: The law provides for the granting of asylum or refugee status. The government has an established refugee protection system but did not effectively implement it. UNHCR recognized more than 600 asylum seekers, while the government recognized only 26. Of the more than 300 asylum-seeker

cases since 2012 that received a final decision, the government rejected 99 percent with the indefinite justification of "failure of proof." NGOs concluded that this alone was evidence of systemic discrimination, as 99 percent of asylum seekers were also of Haitian origin.

The National Office of Refugees in the Migration Directorate of the National Commission for Refugees (CONARE) adjudicates asylum claims. CONARE is an interagency commission that includes the Foreign Ministry, the National Department of Investigations, and General Directorate of Migration. The full commission has the responsibility for making the final decision on individual asylum applications.

A 2013 CONARE resolution requires individuals to apply for asylum within 15 days of arrival in the country. Under this resolution, if an asylum seeker is in the country for more than 15 days and does not apply for asylum, the individual permanently loses the right to apply for asylum. The resolution also rejects as inadmissible any asylum application from an individual who has been in, or proceeds from, a foreign country where the individual could have sought asylum. Thus, the government makes inadmissibility determinations administratively before an asylum interview or evaluation by CONARE.

According to refugee NGOs, there was no information posted at ports of entry to provide notice of the right to seek asylum or of the timeline or process for doing so. Furthermore, these NGOs reported that immigration officials did not know how to handle asylum cases. UNHCR protection officers were occasionally and unpredictably granted access to detained asylum seekers. CONARE policies do not provide for protection screening in the deportation process. By law the government must afford due process to detained asylum seekers, and those expressing a fear of return to their country of nationality or habitual residence should be allowed to apply for asylum under the proper procedures. Nonetheless, there was generally neither judicial review of deportation orders nor any third-party review to provide for protection screening.

CONARE did not provide rejected asylum seekers details of the grounds for the rejection of their initial application for asylum or information regarding the process for appeal. Rejected applicants received a letter informing them that they had 30 days to leave the country voluntarily. Per government policy, rejected asylum seekers have seven days from receipt of notice of denial to file an appeal; however, the letter providing notice of denial does not mention this right to appeal.

<u>Freedom of Movement</u>: Starting in 2015, approved refugees were issued travel documents by the government for a fee of 3,150 pesos ($70). Refugees commented that the travel document listed their nationality as "refugee" and not their country of origin. Asylum seekers with pending cases had only a paper letter to present to avoid deportation, which deterred freedom of movement.

<u>Employment</u>: The government prohibited asylum seekers with pending cases from working. This situation was further complicated by the long, sometimes indefinite, periods of pending cases. Lack of documentation also precluded refugees from certain employment. Employment was nonetheless a requirement for the government to renew refugees' temporary residency cards.

<u>Access to Basic Services</u>: Approved refugees receive the same rights and responsibilities as legal migrants with temporary residence permits. This provided refugees the right to access education, employment, health care, and other social services. UNHCR reported that, in practice, problems remained. Only those refugees able to afford health insurance were able to access adequate health care. Refugees reported that their government-issued identification numbers were not recognized, and thus they could not access other services, such as opening a bank account or entering service contracts for basic utilities, but instead had to rely on friends or family for such services.

Stateless Persons

Prior to 2010, the constitution bestowed citizenship upon anyone born in the country except children born to diplomats and children born to parents who are "in transit." The 2010 constitution added an additional exception for children born in the country to parents without migratory status. In 2013 the Constitutional Tribunal ruled that children born in the country to foreigners "in transit" were not Dominican citizens. In effect the ruling retroactively revised the country's citizenship transmission laws and stripped citizenship from approximately 135,000 persons, mostly the children of undocumented Haitian migrants, who had conferred citizenship by virtue of jus soli since 1929.

Until 2012 the Haitian constitution did not permit dual citizenship. Therefore, individuals of Haitian descent who obtained Dominican citizenship at birth by virtue of birth on Dominican soil forfeited their right to Haitian citizenship. The 2013 Constitutional Tribunal ruling therefore stripped nearly all of those affected of the only citizenship they held.

The Inter-American Commission on Human Rights (IACHR), UNHCR, and the Caribbean Community criticized the 2013 Constitutional Tribunal judgment. The IACHR found that the 2013 tribunal ruling implied an arbitrary deprivation of citizenship and that the ruling had a discriminatory effect, stripped citizenship retroactively, and led to statelessness for individuals not considered citizens.

In May 2014 President Medina signed and promulgated law 169-14, "the Special Status of Individuals born in the territory with an irregular registration in the Civil Registry and on Naturalization." Law 169-14 proposes to regularize and (re)issue identity documents to individuals born in the country between June 16, 1929, and April 18, 2007, to undocumented migrant parents, who were previously registered in the civil registry (Group A), recognizing them as Dominican citizens from birth. Based on an audit of the national civil registry archives, that population was estimated to total 60,000. The law also creates a special path to citizenship for persons born to undocumented migrant parents who never registered in the civil registry, including an estimated 45,000-75,000 undocumented persons, predominantly of Haitian descent (Group B). Group B individuals may apply for legal residency under this law and apply for naturalized citizenship after two years. The law granted Group B individuals 180 days to apply for legal residency, an application window that closed on January 31, 2015. A total of 8,755 Group B individuals successfully applied before that deadline. As of November 2015, the government approved 6,262 cases and continued processing the remainder. NGOs and foreign governments expressed concern for the potentially large number of Group B persons who did not apply within the deadline. The government committed to resolve any unregistered Group B cases but had not identified the legal framework under which that commitment would be fulfilled. The government also committed not to deport anyone born in the country.

In June 2015 the civil registry (known as the Central Electoral Board or JCE) announced it had transferred the civil records of the 54,307 individuals identified in Group A to a separate civil registry book and annulled their original civil registrations. The JCE invited those on the list to report to JCE offices and receive a reissued birth certificate. The vast majority of persons on the list were of Haitian descent. In late 2015 civil society groups reported that many Group A individuals experienced difficulties in obtaining reissued birth certificates at JCE offices. NGOs also documented cases of individuals who they determined qualified as Group A, but who were not included in the JCE's audit results list. In response the government unveiled a number of new mechanisms to facilitate issuance of nationality documentation to Group A. The government also announced new channels for reporting delays or failures to issue Group A nationality documents in

JCE satellite offices around the country, including a telephone line and social media accounts. NGOs reported early in the year that these measures led to improved document issuance rates for Group A but noted that some JCE offices continued to deny issuance to some fully qualified Group A citizenship applicants.

A 2012 National Statistics Office and UN Population Fund study estimated the total Haitian population in the country at 668,145, of whom 458,233 were identified as Haitian immigrants and 209,912 were categorized as persons of Haitian descent. The exact number of undocumented persons remained unclear.

Dominican-born persons of Haitian descent without citizenship or identity documents faced obstacles traveling both within and outside the country. In addition, undocumented persons may not obtain national identification cards or voting cards. Persons who did not have a national identification card or birth certificate had limited access to electoral participation, formal-sector jobs, public education, marriage and birth registration, formal financial services such as banks and loans, courts and judicial procedures, and ownership of land or property.

On September 25, a human rights lawyer who worked on prominent cases of Dominicans of Haitian descent affected by the Constitutional Tribunal judgment was followed from his work, taunted for defending Haitians, and assaulted with a concrete block, leading to the lawyer's hospitalization. Amnesty International reported a trend of verbal and physical attacks on others working on this issue.

Section 3. Freedom to Participate in the Political Process

The law provides citizens the ability to choose their government in free and fair periodic elections conducted by secret ballot based on nearly universal and equal suffrage and guaranteeing the free expression of the will of the people. Per the constitution, active-duty police and military personnel may not vote or participate in partisan political activity.

Elections and Political Participation

Recent Elections: On May 15, voters participated in general elections for all levels of government and elected Danilo Medina of the PLD as president for a second four-year term. According to the JCE, more than 69 percent of the electorate voted. The JCE instituted a new system of electronic vote counting during this election. According to international observers and experts on electronic voting systems, the JCE did not follow international standards, as it neither audited nor gradually implemented the system. In response to doubts about the new system, several opposition political parties publicly and formally complained to the JCE, but the JCE did not respond directly to their complaints. On election day many electronic voting systems failed or remained unused. The JCE had previously used an accurate and efficient manual count system, which many voting centers used instead of the new electronic system. The various vote-counting procedures confused results, such that the JCE did not announce final, official results with all ballots counted until 13 days after the elections. Many congressional and municipal races remained contested for weeks after, leading to sporadic protests and violence. On election day the Organization of American States (OAS) and domestic observers noted widespread political campaigning immediately outside of voting centers in violation of the law, as well indications of vote buying.

Political Parties and Political Participation: The OAS and domestic NGOs criticized the inequality of the preceding political campaigns. As dictated by law, major parties, defined as those that received 5 percent of the vote or more in the previous elections, received 80 percent of public campaign finances, while minor parties had to share the remaining 20 percent of public funds. A domestic NGO pointed to large increases in government spending on advertising in the months leading up to the elections to criticize the government and incumbent PLD party for using public funds to fund their campaign, which is expressly prohibited by law. According to civil society groups, the incumbent PLD party also used public funds, in addition to public campaign funds, to pay for advertising. During the first trimester of 2016, during the height of the elections campaign, the government and the PLD, ranked number two and three, respectively, behind Claro, the nation's largest telecom company, in terms of advertising expenditures. According to election monitors, in 2015 the government spent more than 10 million pesos ($220,000) per day on average on advertising. In the first months of 2016, that figure climbed to more than 14 million pesos ($310,000) per day, and the Office of the President's publicity budget increased more than 300 percent. Similar increases occurred throughout other government ministries. This spending decreased after President Medina ordered a stop to the use of public funds for the campaign in March. According to civil society groups, this revenue in turn influenced the few media conglomerates and encouraged them to censor voices in disagreement with their largest client, the incumbent PLD party.

Participation of Women and Minorities: No laws limit the participation of women in the political process, and they did participate. The JCE instituted several measures to increase voter participation, including access for voters with disabilities, voting at home, and presidential voting in prisons. The JCE reported that at least 104 persons with disabilities voted from home, but domestic and international observers still observed obstacles to access to voting centers. The voting in prison initiative resulted in 1,579 prisoners voting. Nearly all of those affected by the 2013 Constitutional Tribunal ruling were unable to vote in the May elections, as the majority of Group A individuals did not begin receiving citizenship documents under law 169-14 until after the voter registration deadline of January 16, 2016. The identification cards issued clearly stated "No Vote 2016."

Section 4. Corruption and Lack of Transparency in Government

The law provides criminal penalties for official corruption; however, the government did not implement the law effectively, and officials frequently engaged in corrupt practices with impunity. The attorney general investigated allegedly corrupt officials but did not secure any convictions against high-level officials. Government corruption remained a serious problem and public grievance.

The Public Ministry, led by the attorney general, was responsible for investigating and prosecuting corruption cases through the Office of the Special Attorney for the Prosecution of Administrative Corruption (PEPCA). The Chamber of Accounts supported government accountability through audits and investigations, which formed the basis of many PEPCA corruption cases. PEPCA, the Chamber of Accounts, and comptroller general operated independently and appeared free from political influence. While government agencies complained of insufficient resources, credible NGOs noted the greatest hindrance to effective investigations was a lack of political will to apply the law and prosecute particularly high-level politicians.

Corruption: Civil society organizations criticized the widespread practice of awarding government positions as political patronage and alleged many civil servants did not have to perform any job functions for their salary. Small municipalities reported having staffs far in excess of what the physical offices could house.

NGOs as well as average citizens regularly reported that police officers attempted to solicit bribes during routine traffic stops or arrests. Numerous individuals reported having their personal property taken by police. Police reportedly detained drivers, including foreign tourists, and requested money in exchange for release. Local human rights observers reported immigration officials and police officers particularly targeted undocumented immigrants of Haitian descent to extort money by threatening deportation. NGOs reported incidents of corruption among military and immigration officials stationed at border posts and checkpoints.

Prison officials accepted money in exchange for recommendations to release prisoners for health reasons. There were credible allegations that prisoners paid bribes to obtain early release on parole.

The government on occasion used nonjudicial sanctions to punish corruption, including dismissal or transfer of military personnel, police officers, judges, and other minor officials engaged in bribe taking and other corrupt behavior. Widespread acceptance and tolerance of petty corruption, however, hampered anticorruption efforts.

On September 8, the Supreme Court dismissed the corruption case against former minister of public works Victor Diaz Rua, citing lack of evidence. The Diaz Rua case had been pending for two years after a detailed government audit revealed financial mismanagement and millions of dollars in unauthorized bonuses.

Financial Disclosure: The law requires the president, vice president, members of congress, some agency heads, and other officials, including tax and customs duty collectors, to declare their personal property within 30 days of being hired, elected, or re-elected as well as when they end their responsibilities. The constitution further requires public officials to declare the provenance of their property. The law makes the Chamber of Accounts responsible for receiving and reviewing these declarations. As of October, 1,028 public officials had complied with the law, while another 2,058 had not. Transparency NGOs questioned the veracity of the declarations, as amounts often fluctuated significantly year to year, and total declared assets often appeared unrealistically low.

Public Access to Information: The constitution provides for public access to government information. The law places limits on the availability of such information only under specified circumstances, such as to protect national security. Authorities are required to disclose or respond to requests for access within 15 workdays, and processing requests is either free or the fee is reasonable. The law provides for penalties of up to two years in prison and a five-year ban from positions of public trust for officials who obstruct access to public information. Responses to requests were often timely but incomplete, and the government regularly rejected follow-up requests. Although much information was easily available online, it was often inaccurate or inconsistent with other government reports.

Section 5. Governmental Attitude Regarding International and Nongovernmental Investigation of Alleged Violations of Human Rights

A number of domestic and international organizations generally operated without government restriction, investigating and publishing their findings on human rights cases. While officials often were cooperative and responsive, human rights groups that advocated for the rights of Haitians and persons of Haitian descent were an exception and faced occasional government obstruction. On January 8, in an unprecedented gesture, the Ministry of Foreign Affairs and JCE met with a large group of NGOs from across the country that advocate for the rights of Dominicans of Haitian descent. Despite a public commitment to do so, the government did not hold a subsequent meeting.

Government Human Rights Bodies: The constitution establishes the position of human rights ombudsman, and in 2013 the Senate appointed Zoila Martinez, former Santo Domingo district attorney, for a six-year term. The ombudsman's functions as outlined in the constitution are to safeguard the fundamental human rights of persons and to protect collective interests established in the constitution and law. The Interinstitutional Human Rights Commission is chaired by the minister of foreign affairs and the attorney general. The commission did not meet regularly. The Attorney General's Office has its own human rights division.

Section 6. Discrimination, Societal Abuses, and Trafficking in Persons

Women

Rape and Domestic Violence: The law criminalizes violence against women, including rape, incest, sexual aggression, and other forms of domestic violence. Penalties for conviction of these crimes range from one to 30 years in prison and fines from 700 to 245,000 pesos ($15 to $5,400). The sentences for conviction of rape, including spousal rape, range from 10 to 15 years in prison and a fine of 100,000 to 200,000 pesos ($2,210 to $4,420). For rape cases involving a vulnerable person or a child or occurring under other egregious circumstances, the sentence for conviction is 10 to 20 years in prison.

Rape was a serious and pervasive problem. Survivors of rape often did not report the crime due to fear of social stigma, fear of retribution, and the perception that police and the judicial system would not provide redress. The state may prosecute a suspect for rape, including spousal rape, even if the victim does not file charges. Police generally encouraged rape victims to seek assistance from the specialized gender-based violence unit of the National Police, the Attorney General's Office, public defenders, or NGOs.

Despite government efforts to improve the situation, violence against women was pervasive. The National Police reported that 54 women were killed by their partners through July. The Attorney General's Office reported that on average 6,000 women were victims of sexual assault each year. The Attorney General's Office reported it had received more than 500,000 complaints of gender-based or sexual violence, with complaints increasing approximately 33 percent annually. The Attorney General's Office also reported that the caseload far exceeded prosecutorial capacity, such that only a small fraction of these complaints went to court.

The Attorney General's Office oversees the specialized Violence Prevention and Attention Unit, which had 18 offices in the country's 32 provinces. At these offices victims of violence could file criminal complaints, obtain free legal counsel, and receive psychological and medical attention. Each office had professional psychologists on staff to counsel victims and to assess the threat of impending danger associated with a complaint. These offices had the authority to issue a temporary restraining order immediately after receiving a complaint.

In an additional step to address the problem, the Attorney General's Office instructed its officers not to settle cases of violence against women and to continue judicial processes, even in cases in which victims withdrew charges. District attorneys provided assistance and protection to victims of violence by referring them to appropriate institutions for legal, medical, and psychological counseling. The Attorney General's Office also instructed its officers to conclude the investigation and presentation of charges within 35 days unless the case was considered complex.

The Office for the Attention of Women and Interfamily Violence, headed by Colonel Teresa Martinez, managed emergency call lines to facilitate quick response services. The office had a trained police officer in six of the 17 satellite violence-prevention and attention-unit offices.

The Ministry of Women, which had scarce resources, actively promoted equality and the prevention of violence against women through implementing education and awareness programs and the provision of training to other ministries and offices. The ministry operated two shelters for domestic violence survivors in undisclosed locations, where abused persons could make reports to police and receive counseling. The shelters provided women with short- and medium-term assistance of up to three months to escape violent situations, although the high demand limited stays to 15 days. The ministry had a presence in 31 provincial offices and 21 municipal offices, where it offered free legal counsel and psychiatric assistance to victims. The ministry also operated two programs to rehabilitate persons convicted of domestic abuse or gender-based violence. Through April the shelters had received 237 women; however, with a capacity of only 25 women and children at a time, the shelters were not able to accept all victims.

NGOs stated that while adequate laws were in place to punish gender-based violence, the judicial system did not adequately enforce those laws. The system lacked an integrated approach to victim care, the judicial system lacked the resources to prosecute perpetrators successfully, and the number of women's shelters was inadequate for victim's needs.

Sexual Harassment: Sexual harassment in the workplace is a misdemeanor, and conviction carries a sentence of one year in prison and a fine equal to the sum of three to six months of salary. Union leaders reported, however, that the law was not enforced and that sexual harassment remained a problem (see section 7.d.).

Reproductive Rights: Couples and individuals have the right to decide the number, spacing, and timing of their children; manage their reproductive health; and have access to the means and information to do so free from discrimination, coercion, and violence. Family-planning NGOs provided contraceptives without charge. Many low-income women, however, used them inconsistently due to irregular availability and societal influences. Religious beliefs and social customs reduced the use of modern methods of family planning. According to 2016 estimates by the UN Fund for Population (UNFPA), 69 percent of women used a modern method of contraception, and 11 percent of women had an unmet need for family planning; unmet need was higher among young women and adolescents (28 percent), and sterilization accounted for nearly half of all methods used, according to UNFPA. UNFPA reported that the adolescent birth rate was also high, at 90 births per 1,000 girls ages 15-19, and 21 percent of adolescents were mothers or pregnant. Although 98 percent of births were attended by skilled health personnel, the maternal mortality was 92 deaths per 100,000 live births, and the lifetime risk of maternal death was one in 400, according to 2015 UN estimates.

Through June the country's maternal hospitals reported that 35 women had died in childbirth. Maternal mortality remained a problem due to medical reasons, including failure to adhere to standards of quality care, general lack of accountability and an insufficient culture of patient safety, inadequate referrals, and residents filling in for attending physicians without sufficient supervision.

A high rate of pregnancies among adolescent girls remained a concern. The country's maternal hospitals reported a 28 percent teenage pregnancy rate. Other significant factors contributing to maternal and neonatal deaths were poor quality of care and lack of access to health-care services as well as complications during pregnancy and delivery. Most women and girls had access to some postnatal care, although the lack of postnatal care was higher among those that were uneducated and from low economic backgrounds as well as young mothers.

Discrimination: Although the law provides women and men the same legal rights, women did not enjoy social and economic status or opportunity equal to that of men. Men held approximately 70 percent of leadership positions in all sectors. Only 11 percent of firms had female top managers. According to the Inter-American Development Bank, on average women received 16 percent lower pay than men in jobs of equal content and requiring equal skills. In 2014 the average unemployment rate among men was 9 percent of the active labor force, while for women it was 23 percent. Some employers reportedly gave pregnancy tests to women before hiring them as part of a required medical examination. Although it is illegal to discriminate based on such tests, NGO leaders reported that employers often did not hire pregnant women and sometimes fired female employees who became pregnant. There were no effective government programs to combat economic discrimination against women.

Children

Birth Registration: Citizenship comes with birth in the country, except to children born to diplomats, to those who are "in transit," or to parents who are illegally in the country (see section 2.d.). A child born abroad to a Dominican mother or father may also acquire citizenship. A child not registered at birth is undocumented until parents file a late declaration of birth. According to the UN Children's Fund (UNICEF), 12 percent of children under the age of five were not legally registered.

Education: The constitution stipulates free, compulsory public education through age 18, however not all children attend. A June report from UNICEF showed 26.8

percent of poor children did not attend primary school, compared with 4.3 percent of middle and upper class children. A birth certificate is required to register for high school, which discouraged some children from attending or completing school, particularly children of Haitian descent affected by the Constitutional Tribunal's 2013 ruling (see section 2.d.). Children who lacked documentation also were restricted from attending secondary school (past the eighth grade) and faced problems accessing other public services.

Child Abuse: Abuse of children, including physical, sexual, and psychological abuse, was a serious problem. In May the attorney general publicly decried the problem of child abuse and stated that his office had already received 2,315 reports of child abuse. The Children and Adolescents Unit of the Attorney General's Office maintained a hotline that persons could call to report cases of child abuse. Cases were often not pursued because of family embarrassment, lack of economic resources, or lack of knowledge regarding available legal assistance. The Santo Domingo district attorney's office reported that, in most abuse cases, the accused was a person close to the child, such as a family member or close family friend. The law provides for removal of a mistreated child to a protective environment.

The law contains provisions concerning child abuse, including physical and emotional mistreatment, sexual exploitation, and child labor. The law provides for sentences of two and five years' incarceration and a fine of three to five times the monthly minimum wage for persons convicted of abuse of a minor. The penalty doubles if the abuse is related to trafficking. The government's National Directorate for Assistance to Victims coordinated the efforts of official entities and NGOs to assist children who were victims of violence and abuse.

Early and Forced Marriage: The legal minimum age for marriage with parental consent is 16 for boys and 15 for girls. Marriage, particularly of women, before the age of 18 was common. According to UNICEF, 10 percent of girls were married by the age of 15 and 37 percent by 18. The government conducted no known prevention or mitigation programs. Girls often married much older men. Child marriage occurred more frequently among girls who were uneducated, poor, and living in rural areas.

Sexual Exploitation of Children: The law defines statutory rape as sexual relations with anyone under the age of 18. Penalties for conviction of statutory rape are 10 to 20 years in prison and a fine of 100,000 to 200,000 pesos ($2,210 to $4,420). The law also contains specific provisions that prohibit child pornography and child prostitution, and prescribe penalties for sexual abuse of children of 20 to 30 years' imprisonment and fines of 100,000 to 200,000 pesos ($2,210 to $4,420).

The press often reported on pedophilia cases. The commercial sexual exploitation of children generally occurred in tourist locations and major urban areas. The government conducted programs to combat the sexual exploitation of minors, including the "House to House" program with UNICEF to educate the most at-risk populations about child sexual exploitation.

Displaced Children: A large population of children, primarily Haitians or Dominicans of Haitian descent, lived on the streets (see section 2.d.). There were reports of Haitian children trafficking victims (see the Department of State's *Trafficking in Persons Report* at www.state.gov/j/tip/rls/tiprpt/).

International Child Abductions: The country is a party to the 1980 Hague Convention on International Child Abduction. See the Department of State's *Annual Report on International Parental Child Abduction* at travel.state.gov/content/childabduction/en/legal/compliance.html.

Anti-Semitism

The Jewish community comprised approximately 350 persons. There were no reports of anti-Semitic acts.

Trafficking in Persons

See the Department of State's *Trafficking in Persons Report* at www.state.gov/j/tip/rls/tiprpt/.

Persons with Disabilities

Although the law prohibits discrimination against persons with physical, sensory, intellectual, and mental disabilities, these individuals encountered discrimination in employment, education, the judicial system, and in obtaining health care and transportation services. The law provides for physical access for persons with disabilities to all new public and private buildings and access to basic services. It also specifies that each ministry should collaborate with the National Disability Council to implement these provisions. Authorities worked to enforce these provisions, but a gap in implementation persisted. Very few public buildings were fully accessible. The Ibero-American Network of Physically Disabled Persons reported that many students who use wheelchairs could not access classrooms due to narrow entrances and lack of ramps.

The Dominican Association for Rehabilitation received support from the Secretariat of Public Health and from the Office of the Presidency to provide rehabilitation assistance to persons with physical and learning disabilities as well as to run schools for children with physical and mental disabilities. Lack of accessible public transportation for persons with disabilities was still a major impediment for the mobility of persons with disabilities.

The law states that the government should provide for persons with disabilities to have access to the labor market as well as to cultural, recreational, and religious activities, but it was not consistently enforced. The Santo Domingo Center for Integrated Care for Children remained the only facility serving children with developmental disabilities. In May the Ministry of Education reported that 80 percent of registered students with disabilities attended school.

National/Racial/Ethnic Minorities

There was evidence of racial prejudice and discrimination against persons of dark complexion, but the government denied such prejudice or discrimination existed and, consequently, did little to address the problem. Prejudice against Haitians disadvantaged Haitians and Dominicans of Haitian descent, as well as other foreigners of dark complexion. Civil society and international organizations reported that officials denied health care and documentation services to persons of Haitian descent. Local NGOs reported incidents where darker-skinned persons were denied access or services in banks, service in restaurants and stores, entry into nightclubs, enrollment in private schools, and birth registration in hospitals. Economic opportunities were also denied to darker-skinned persons, based on the cultural requirement for a "buena presencia" (good appearance).

Acts of Violence, Discrimination, and Other Abuses Based on Sexual Orientation and Gender Identity

Treatment of lesbian, gay, bisexual, transgender, and intersex (LGBTI) individuals ranged from ambivalent tolerance to resolute homophobia. No specific law protects individuals against discrimination based on sexual orientation or gender identity. The constitution provides that the state shall promote matrimony as a union between a man and a woman; however, it does not define marriage to be exclusively between a man and woman. The law does not extend the same rights to cohabiting same-sex couples as to cohabiting heterosexual couples. The law prohibits discrimination based on sexual orientation and gender identity only for policies related to youth and youth development.

NGOs reported widespread discrimination against LGBTI persons, particularly transgender individuals and lesbians, in such areas as health care, education, justice, and employment. LGBTI individuals often faced intimidation and harassment. Although civil society conducted numerous workshops to raise awareness and alter negative public perceptions, Americas Barometer and Latinobarometro polls showed split societal views towards the human rights of LGBTI persons, with a slim majority not in favor of protecting against discrimination. Religious groups held rallies against the LGBTI community. A 2014 Gallup poll found 73 percent of those polled acknowledged societal discrimination against the LGBTI community. Roman Catholic and evangelical religious leaders often publicly criticized LGBTI activists and international organizations that promoted the human rights of LGBTI persons, at times using derogatory terms and insults against prominent LGBTI individuals or activists. In anticipation of the May general elections, the Catholic and evangelical churches published lists of candidates that supported the human rights of LGBTI persons and encouraged followers not to vote for those candidates. The 2016 election cycle was the first with an openly gay candidate for public office. The main opposition candidate for president publicly stated that he was tolerant of all sexual preferences. In May during the OAS General Assembly in Santo Domingo, thousands gathered outside of the venue to protest the alleged OAS agenda of promoting the human rights of LGBTI persons.

NGOs reported police abuse, including arbitrary arrest, police violence, and extortion, against members of the LGBTI community. They also reported that LGBTI persons were reluctant to file official charges or complaints due to fear of reprisals or humiliation. An LGBTI rights NGO reported 36 hate crimes against the LGBTI community through August. In June there were reports of a police effort to break up LGBTI gatherings in Santiago. On June 17, nine members of the LGBTI community were arrested in Colon Park. Those arrested alleged other forms of humiliation and abuse. The prosecutor's office intervened after the nine had been in detention without cause for 24 hours and secured their release. On October 2, police arrested a group of 15 at Duarte Park in Santo Domingo, another public gathering site for the LGBTI community. Again, no specific cause was given for the arrests, and all individuals were released within 24 hours. In both incidents police and prosecutor's offices announced investigations, but no prosecutions resulted from the investigations.

LGBTI persons often gathered informally in public spaces. Formal gatherings generally required the approval of the Community Board of Neighbors, an institution influenced by the Catholic Church and its conservative views on LGBTI issues. On July 3, for the sixth year in a row, the LGBTI community successfully held a gay pride parade and solidarity concert.

HIV and AIDS Social Stigma

The National Council on HIV/AIDS reported that 68,000 individuals or 0.8 percent of the total population had HIV or AIDS. The council further reported that 18 percent of the transgender population had HIV or AIDS. Persons with HIV/AIDS faced discrimination, especially in the workplace.

Persons with HIV/AIDS routinely faced discrimination in access to health care and employment. NGOs reported that health workers discriminated against HIV/AIDS patients, which prevented persons from being tested for HIV/AIDS or receiving preventive services and treatment. Although the law prohibits the use of HIV testing to screen employees, Human Rights Watch, Amnesty International, and the International Labor Organization (ILO) reported that workers in various industries faced obligatory HIV testing. Workers were sometimes tested without their knowledge or consent. Many workers found to have the disease were not hired, and those employed were either fired from their jobs or denied adequate health care. According to the National Council on HIV/AIDS, those with HIV or AIDS were not covered by the country's social security system. The municipality of Boca Chica passed a resolution in June prohibiting discrimination based on HIV or AIDS status but struck sections based on discrimination based on sexual orientation.

The President's Council on AIDS, which included public- and private-sector members and persons who were HIV/AIDS positive, coordinated policy at the national level and cooperated with local NGOs to reduce the impact of HIV/AIDS on vulnerable populations and society. The Ministry of Health also funded NGOs and private organizations, such as the Center for Orientation and Integration, which worked to combat discrimination and assist with integration into society.

Other Societal Violence or Discrimination

On a number of occasions, citizens attacked and sometimes killed alleged criminals in vigilante-style reprisals for theft, robbery, or burglary. A leading newspaper published a series of reports detailing this trend of vigilantism, citing 64 persons killed between 2013 and 2015 by mob justice. Observers attributed these incidents to an increase in crime and the perceived inability of security forces to stem or combat incidents of crime.

Section 7. Worker Rights

a. Freedom of Association and the Right to Collective Bargaining

The law provides for the right of workers, with the exception of military and police, to form and join independent unions, conduct legal strikes, and bargain collectively; however, it places several restrictions on these rights. For example, a requirement considered excessive by the ILO restricts trade union rights by requiring unions to represent 50 percent plus one of the workers in an enterprise to bargain collectively. In addition, the law prohibits strikes until mandatory mediation requirements have been met. Formal requirements for a strike to be legal also include the support of an absolute majority of all company workers for the strike, written notification to the Ministry of Labor, and a 10-day waiting period following notification before proceeding with the strike. Government workers and essential public service personnel may not strike.

The law prohibits antiunion discrimination and forbids employers from dismissing an employee for participating in union activities, including being part of a committee seeking to form a union. Although the law requires the Ministry of Labor to register unions for them to be legal, it provides for automatic recognition of a union if the ministry has not acted on an application within 30 days. The law allows unions to conduct their activities without government interference. Public-sector workers may form associations registered through the Office of Public Administration. The law requires that 40 percent of civil servant employees agree to join a union in a given government entity for it to be formed. According to the Ministry of Labor, the law applies to all workers, including foreign workers, those working as domestic workers, workers without legal documentation, and workers in the free trade zones (FTZs).

The government inconsistently enforced laws related to freedom of association and collective bargaining. Labor inspectors did not consistently investigate allegations of violations of freedom of association and collective bargaining rights. For example, workers in the sugar sector continued to report that labor inspectors in the sector did not ask workers or supervisors about workers' freedom to associate, right to organize, union membership or activity, or collective bargaining, although workers had separately reported some instances of employers threatening them with firing or loss of housing if they were to meet with coworkers.

Penalties under law for labor practices contrary to freedom of association range from seven to 12 times the minimum wage and may increase by 50 percent if the employer repeats the act. Noncompliance with a collective bargaining agreement is punishable with a fine equaling three to six times the minimum wage. Such fines were insufficient to deter employers from violating worker rights and were rarely enforced. In addition, the process for dealing with disputes through labor courts was often long, with cases pending for several years. NGOs and labor federations reported companies took advantage of the slow and ineffective legal system to appeal cases, which left workers without labor rights protection in the interim.

The government and private sector did not consistently respect freedom of association and the right to collective bargaining. There were reports of intimidation, threats, and blackmail by employers to prevent union activity. Some unions required members to provide legal documentation to participate in the union, despite the fact that the labor code protects all workers within the territory regardless of their legal status. Dominican air traffic controllers claimed they were fired for engaging in union activity and filed a lawsuit. The lower court decision ordering the reinstatement of the controllers was overturned on appeal.

Labor NGOs reported the majority of companies resisted collective negotiating practices and union activities. Companies reportedly fired workers for union activity and blacklisted trade unionists, among other antiunion practices. Workers frequently had to sign documents pledging to abstain from participating in union activities. Companies also created and supported "yellow" or company-backed unions to counter free and democratic unions. Formal strikes occurred but were not common.

Companies used short-term contracts and subcontracting, which made union organizing and collective bargaining more difficult. Few companies had collective bargaining pacts, partly because companies created obstacles to union formation and could afford to go through lengthy judicial processes that nascent unions could not afford.

The Dominican Federation of Free Trade Zone Workers (FEDOTRAZONAS) reported that the management of several companies or their subcontractors conducted antiunion campaigns within their enterprises, which included threats to fire union members, and engaged in activities to forestall attainment of union membership sufficient to establish collective bargaining rights under the labor code. The Ministry of Labor intervened in some cases to provide mediation.

Unions in the FTZs reported that their members hesitated to discuss union activity at work due to fear of losing their jobs. Unions accused some FTZ companies of discharging workers who attempted to organize unions.

NGOs continued to report that many Haitian laborers and Dominicans of Haitian descent in construction and agricultural industries, including sugar, did not exercise their rights due to fear of firing or deportation. The Ministry of Labor reported that, during the first half of 2014, there were 237,843 Haitians living in the country, of whom 157,562 were working in the formal and informal sectors of the economy. Multiple labor unions represented Haitians working in the formal sector; however, these unions were not influential. The ministry also stated that Haitians earned, on average, 60 percent of what a Dominican worker received in wages.

b. Prohibition of Forced or Compulsory Labor

The law prohibits all forms of forced or compulsory labor. The law prescribes penalties for conviction of forced labor of up to 20 years' imprisonment with fines; such penalties were sufficiently stringent to deter abuses.

The government reported it received no forced labor complaints during the year. Nonetheless, there were credible reports of forced labor of adults in the service, construction, and agricultural sectors as well as reports of forced labor of children. (see section 7.c.). For example, workers and unions reported instances of forced overtime, induced indebtedness, deception, false promises about terms of work, and withholding and nonpayment of wages in the construction and agricultural sectors, including sugar.

Haitian workers' lack of documentation and legal status in the country made them vulnerable to forced labor. Although specific data on the problem were limited, Haitian nationals reportedly endured forced labor in the service, construction, and agricultural sectors. Many of the 240,000 mostly Haitian irregular migrants who received temporary (one- or two-year) legal residency through the Regularization Plan for Foreigners worked in these sectors. In 2015 and 2016, the government created the regulatory framework to include documented migrants in the national social security network, including disability, health-care, and retirement benefits. As of November the government had not started providing these benefits.

Also see the Department of State's *Trafficking in Persons Report* at www.state.gov/j/tip/rls/tiprpt.

c. Prohibition of Child Labor and Minimum Age for Employment

The law prohibits employment of children under the age of 14 and places restrictions on the employment of children under the age of 16, limiting their working hours to six hours per day. For those under the age of 18, the law limits night work and prohibits employment in dangerous work, such as work involving hazardous substances, heavy or dangerous machinery, and carrying heavy loads. The law also prohibits minors from selling alcohol, certain work in the hotel industry, handling cadavers, and various tasks involved in the production of sugarcane, such as planting, cutting, carrying, and lifting sugarcane, or handling the bagasse. Firms employing underage children are subject to fines and legal sanctions.

The Ministry of Labor, in coordination with the National Council for Children and Adolescents (CONANI), is responsible for enforcing child labor laws. While the ministry and CONANI generally effectively enforced regulations in the formal sector, child labor in the informal sector was a problem. The law provides penalties for child labor violations, including fines and prison sentences.

A National Steering Committee against Child Labor plan to eliminate the worst forms of child labor set objectives, identified priorities, and assigned responsibilities to combat exploitative child labor. Several government programs focused on preventing child labor in coffee, tomato, and rice production; street vending; domestic labor; and commercial sexual exploitation.

The government continued to implement a project with the ILO to remove 100,000 children and adolescents from exploitative labor as part of its Roadmap towards the Elimination of Child Labor. The roadmap aimed to eliminate the worst forms of child labor in the country and all other types of child labor by 2020.

Nevertheless, child labor remained a problem. A health survey published by the National Statistics Office revealed that 12.8 percent of children between the ages of five and 17 performed some sort of illegal child labor.

Child labor occurred primarily in the informal economy, small businesses, private households, and the agricultural sector. In particular there were reports children worked in the production of garlic, potatoes, coffee, sugarcane, tomatoes, and rice. Children often accompanied their parents to work in agricultural fields. NGOs also reported many children worked in the service sector in a number of jobs, including as domestic servants, street vendors and beggars, shoe shiners, and car window washers. The commercial sexual exploitation of children remained a problem, especially in popular tourist destinations and urban areas (see section 6, Children).

Many children who worked as domestic servants were victims of forced labor. There were credible reports that poor Haitian families arranged for Dominican families to "adopt" their children. In some cases adoptive parents reportedly did not treat the children as full family members, expecting them to work in the household or family businesses rather than attend school, which resulted in a kind of indentured servitude for children and adolescents. There were also reports of forced labor of children in street vending and begging, agriculture, construction, and moving of illicit narcotics.

Also see the Department of Labor's *Findings on the Worst Forms of Child Labor* at www.dol.gov/ilab/reports/child-labor/findings.

d. Discrimination with Respect to Employment and Occupation

The law prohibits all forms of discrimination, exclusion, or preference in employment based on gender, age, language, race, color, nationality, social origin, disability, political or union affiliation, religious belief, and against persons with HIV/AIDS. There is no law against discrimination in employment based on sexual orientation.

The government did not effectively enforce the laws against discrimination in employment. Discrimination in employment and occupation occurred with respect to LGBTI persons, especially transgender persons; against HIV/AIDS-positive persons; and against persons with disabilities, persons of darker skin color, and women (see section 6). For example, the ILO noted its concern regarding continued sexual harassment in the workplace and urged the government to take specific steps to address existing social and cultural stereotypes contributing to discrimination. Discrimination against Haitian migrant workers and Dominicans of Haitian descent occurred across sectors. Many Haitian irregular migrants did not have full access to benefits, including social security and health care (see sections 7.b. and 7.e.).

In August 2015 the Ministry of Labor announced a campaign against labor discrimination, "Let's All Work from Equality." The program provided support to vulnerable groups, including persons with disabilities, women, those with a different sexual orientation, and individuals with HIV/AIDS.

e. Acceptable Conditions of Work

There were 14 different minimum wages, depending on the industry. The minimum wage for workers in FTZs was 8,310 pesos ($183) per month. The minimum wage for workers outside the zones ranged from 7,843 pesos ($173) to 12,873 pesos ($284) per month. The minimum wage for the public sector was 5,884 pesos ($130) per month. The daily minimum wage for agricultural workers was 234 pesos ($5.17) based on a 10-hour day, with the exception of sugarcane field workers, who received 146 pesos ($3.22) based on an eight-hour workday. Minimum wage provisions cover all workers, including migrants. The Central Bank calculated that, due to inflation, the minimum wage had not increased in real terms since 1979. The Worker Rights Consortium and labor confederations estimated the living wage was 27,897 pesos ($616) per month.

In 2012 the Ministry of Economy, Planning, and Development used 2007 statistics to calculate the official poverty line at 3,247 pesos ($72) per month. The ministry stated that 43 percent of the population was living in poverty. In February 2015 the Juan Bosch Foundation released a study that reported 63 percent of working Dominicans did not receive an income sufficient to pay for the lowest-cost family budget, and only 3.4 percent received a salary adequate to provide for a family of four. The report stated that 80 percent of workers earned less than 20,000 pesos ($454) per month.

In August 2015 the National Salary Commission approved a 15.5 percent wage increase for construction workers. The Ministry of Labor stated that the increase would benefit all construction workers throughout the country. The National Salary Commission agreed on the increase after hearing the arguments presented by the National Federation of Construction Workers as well as by representatives from the private construction sector.

The Ministry of Labor, in a tripartite agreement with unions and the private sector, approved a 14 percent private-sector minimum wage increase in May 2015. The minimum wage last increased during the 1990s. A random survey conducted by a major daily newspaper found that, although the majority of those polled approved of the increase, most stated the increase would not improve their well-being. Trade unions, which sought an increase of 28 to 30 percent, reported dissatisfaction with the outcome of the tripartite negotiation.

The law establishes a standard workweek of 44 hours. While agricultural workers are exempt from this limit, in no case may the workday exceed 10 hours. The law stipulates all workers be entitled to 36 hours of uninterrupted rest each week. Although the law provides for paid annual holidays and premium pay for overtime, enforcement was ineffective. The law prohibits excessive or compulsory overtime and states that employees may work a maximum of 80 hours of overtime during three months. The labor code covers domestic workers but does not provide for notice or severance payments. Domestic workers are entitled to two weeks' paid vacation after one year of continuous work as well as a Christmas bonus equal to one month's wage. The labor code also covers workers in the FTZs, but they are not entitled to bonus payments.

The Ministry of Labor sets workplace safety and health regulations. By regulation employers are obligated to provide for the safety and health of employees in all aspects related to the job. By law employees may remove themselves from situations that endanger health or safety without jeopardy to their employment, but in practice they could not do so without reprisal.

Authorities did not always enforce minimum wage, hours of work, and workplace health and safety standards. Penalties for these violations range between three and six times the minimum wage. Both the Social Security Institute and the Ministry of Labor had a small corps of inspectors charged with enforcing labor standards. The ministry reported in 2015 that it trained labor inspectors on inspection protocols and best practices and conducted outreach campaigns for workers and employers that focused on labor rights and duties, enrollment in social security, work contracts, and child labor.

Workers complained that labor inspectors lacked training, did not respond to their complaints, and responded to requests from employers more quickly than requests from workers. In the sugar sector, for example, there continued to be reports of procedural and methodological shortcomings in the ministry's inspections, such as: interviewing few or no workers, failing to discuss topics related to law compliance with workers, conducting worker interviews with employer representatives present, employing inspectors with language skills (particularly Creole) insufficient for effective communication with all workers, failing to follow up on allegations of violations made by workers during the inspection process, and failing to conduct follow-up inspections to verify remediation of identified violations. FEDOTRAZONAS reported that the government did not sufficiently monitor workplace safety and health regulations and did not sanction identified violations.

Mandatory overtime was a common practice in factories, enforced through loss of pay or employment for those who refused. FEDOTRAZONAS reported that some companies set up "four-by-four" work schedules, under which employees worked 12-hour shifts for four days. In some cases employees working the four-by-four schedules were not paid overtime for hours worked in excess of maximum work hours allowed under labor laws. Some companies continued the practice of paying every eight days, a biweekly salary with the four-by-four schedules, instead of every seven days, a weekly salary with a standard 44-hour schedule. These practices resulted in underpayment of wages for workers, as they were not compensated for the extra hours worked.

According to an ILO report published in 2014, informal employment as a portion of nonagricultural employment grew from 50 percent in 2011 to 51.5 percent in 2012. In 2013 the Central Bank calculated that 58 percent of employment was informal and theorized the high rate stemmed from a low minimum wage and workforce elasticity in the availability of cheap migrant labor. Workers in the informal economy faced more precarious working conditions than formal workers and were often outside the reach of government enforcement efforts.

Conditions for agricultural workers were poor. Many workers worked long hours, often 12 hours per day and seven days per week, and suffered from hazardous working conditions, including exposure to pesticides, long periods in the sun, and sharp and heavy tools. Some workers reported they were not paid the legally mandated minimum wage.

Companies did not regularly adhere to workplace safety and health regulations. For example, the National Confederation of Trade Unions Unity reported unsafe and inadequate health and safety conditions, including lack of appropriate work attire and safety gear; vehicles without airbags, first aid kits, properly functioning windows, or air conditioning; inadequate ventilation in workspaces; an insufficient number of bathrooms; and unsafe eating areas.

Accidents caused injury and death to workers, but information on the number of accidents was unavailable by year's end.

www.ingramcontent.com/pod-product-compliance
Lightning Source LLC
Chambersburg PA
CBHW080818280726
48660CB00018B/3517